The Best HUMOR of ...

Tiritilli

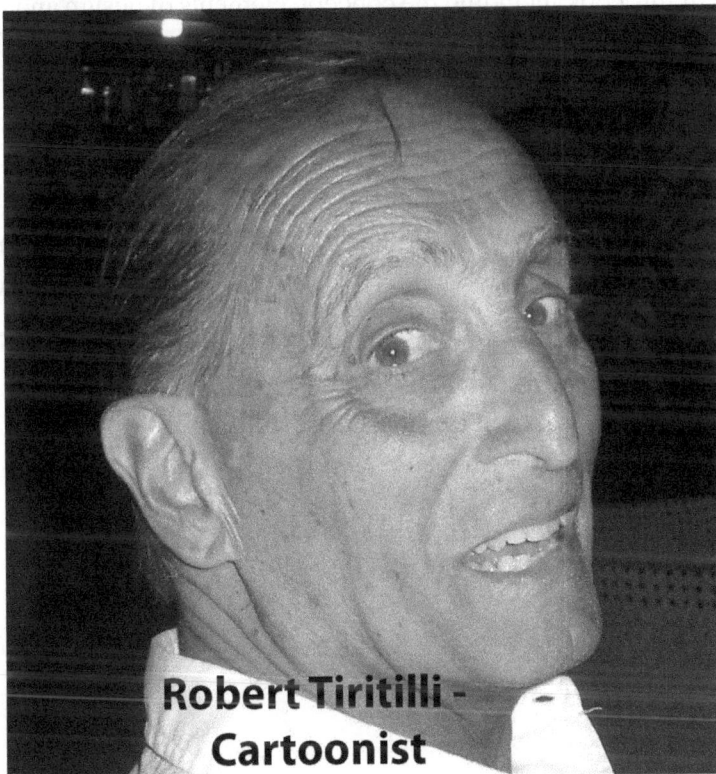

Robert Tiritilli -
Cartoonist

ISBN 978-0-935938-64-7
Illustrations by Robert A.Tiritilli
Cover & Interior Design by Charles S. Hellman
Edited by Charles S. Hellman

"You can play any position you want!"

"The best club in his bag is a PENCIL"

"You're kinda mushie after thawing out."

"Bet on number "2"
across the board, huh?"

"You dummy, how could you flunk your driver license test?"

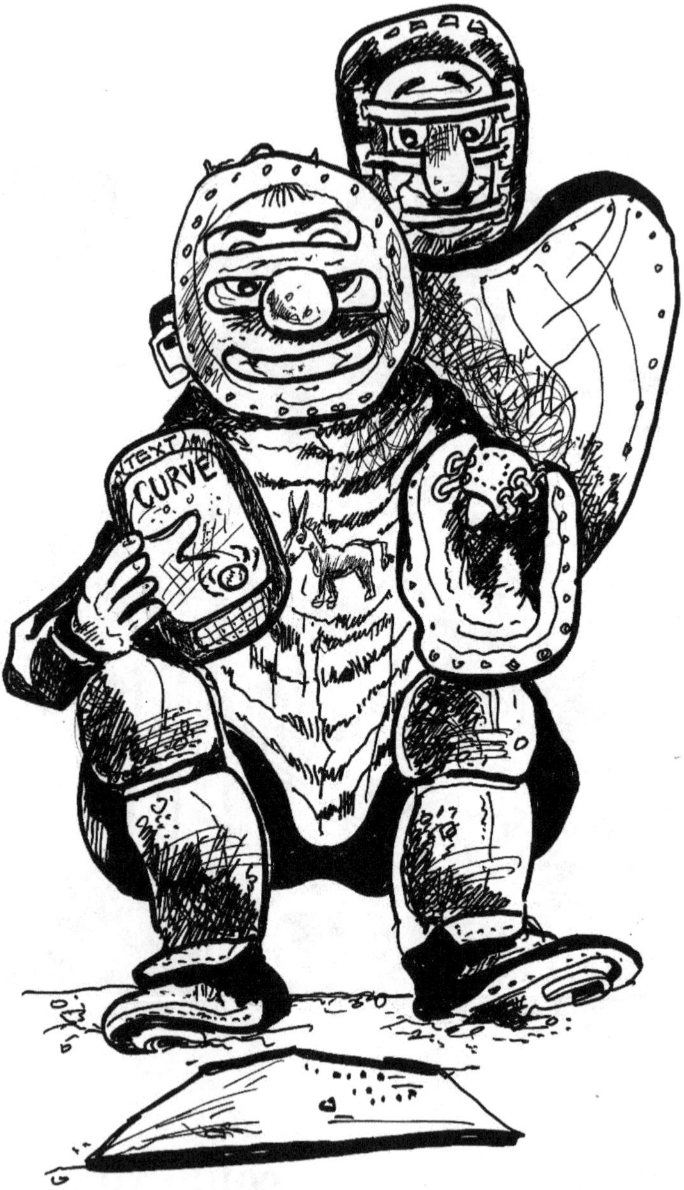
TEXT
CURVE

Signaling the pitcher

Alexander Bell calling his bookie.

"Have you ever heard of a GLUE FACTORY?"

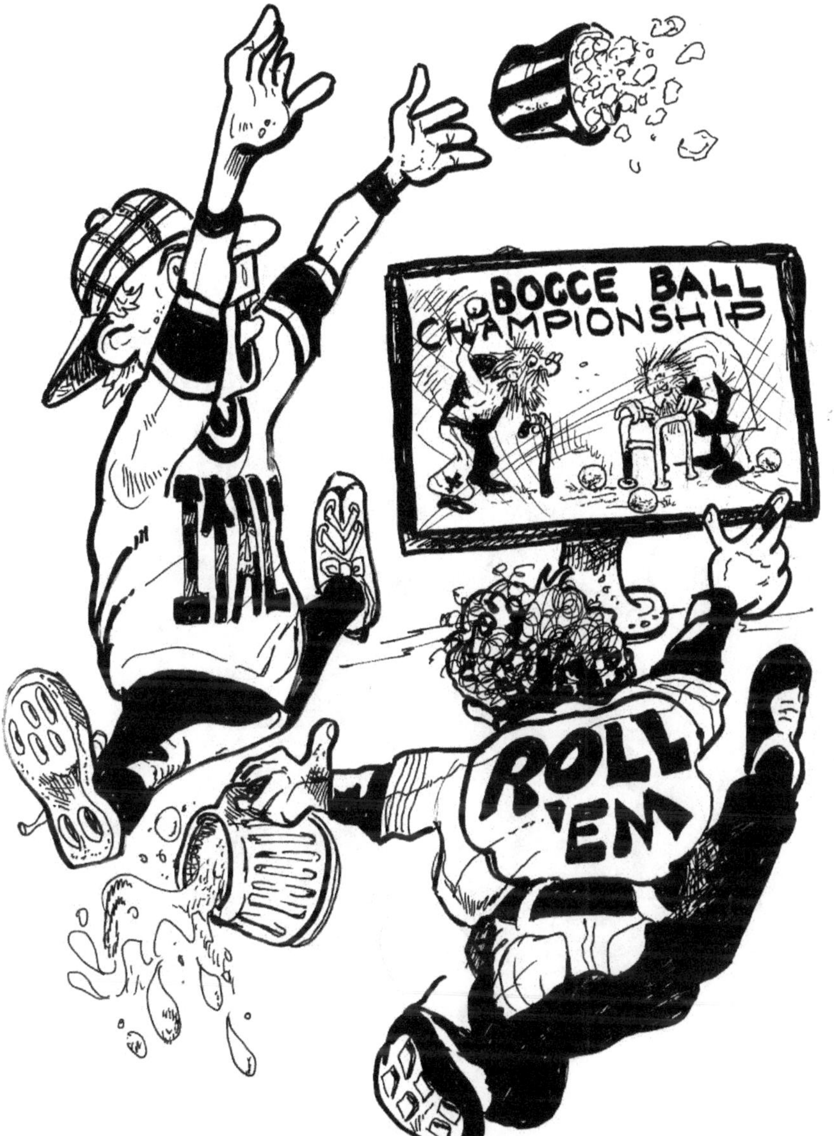
BOCCE BALL
CHAMPIONSHIP
ITAL
ROLL
'EM

Kissing the Pallino

"I only play players with odd numbers on their jerseys!"

"He used to be a brain surgeon."

"Can you believe I am the new football poster boy!"

Bad news: Spring training camp switched from regular beer to light beer.

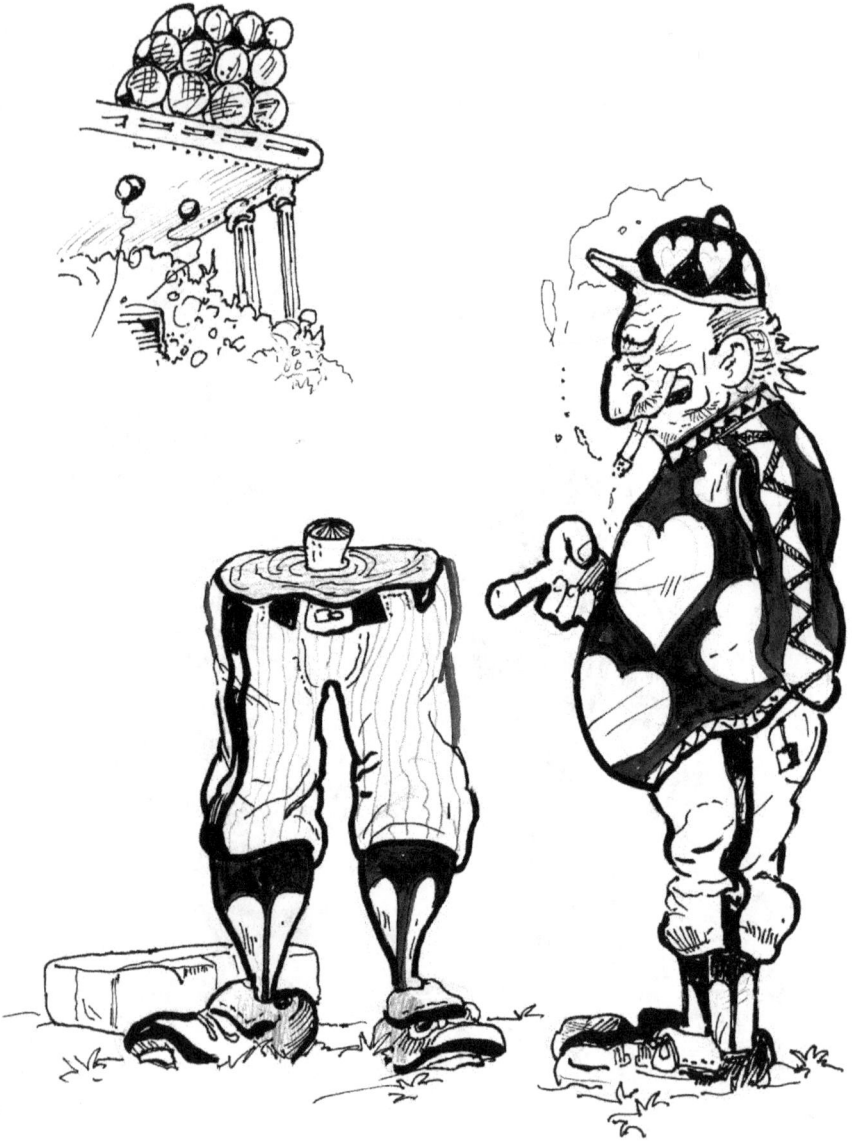

"You're the perfect cut-off man."

"You bet on the wrong team!"

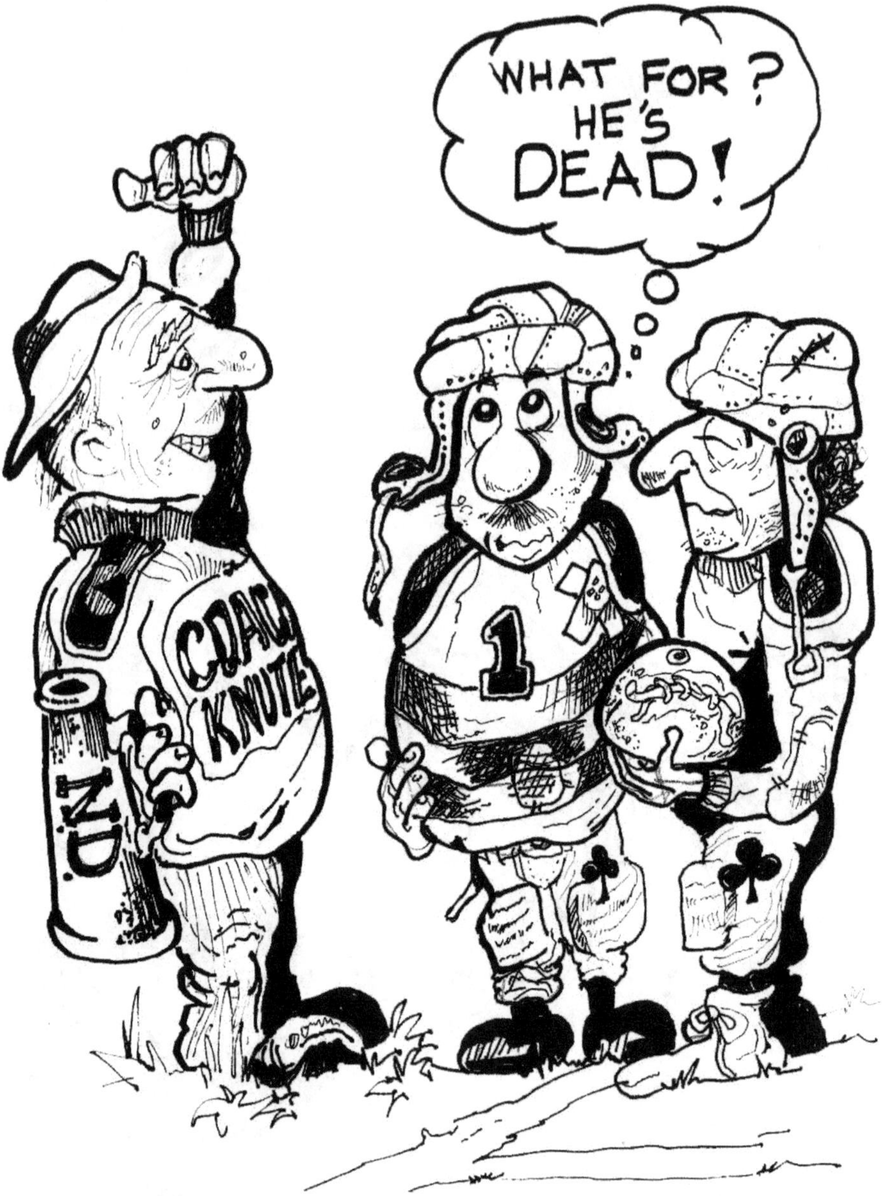
WHAT FOR ? HE'S DEAD!
COACH KNUTE
1
N.D.

"Win one for the GIPPER!"

"I can't believe you got
a speeding ticket."

19

**"Listen you idiot,
there are no bumble bees on the team!"**

"You should hear him when we win."

"Just remember you're the team's clown, not me."

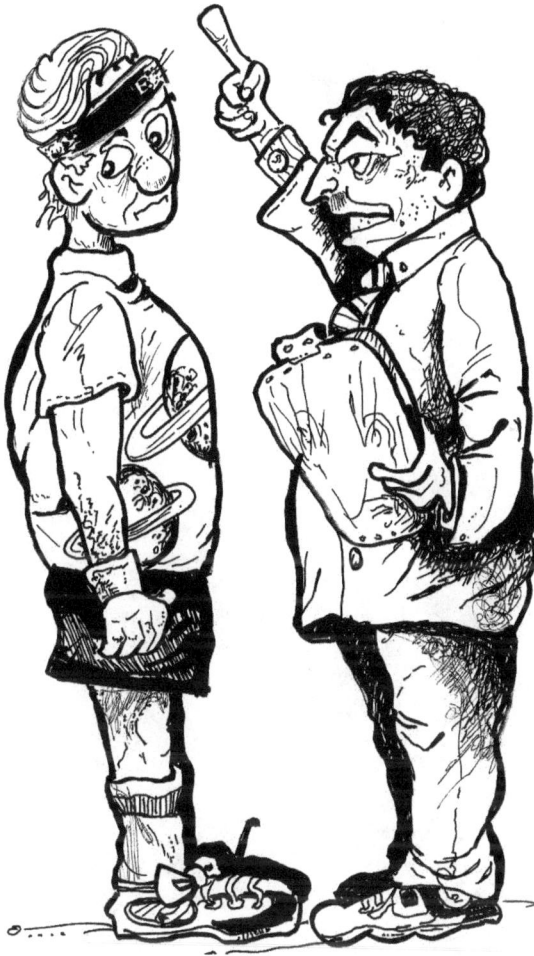

**"One more screw-up
and you're suspended!"**

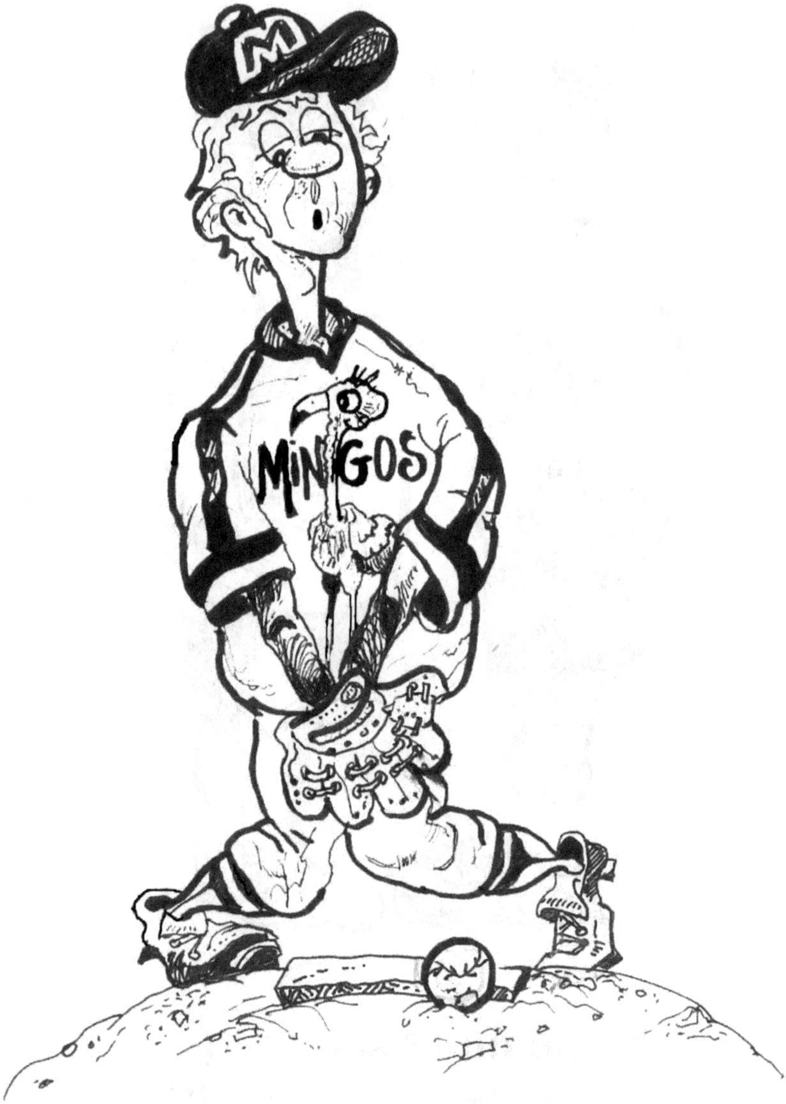
MINGOS

"I have to go pee-pee!"

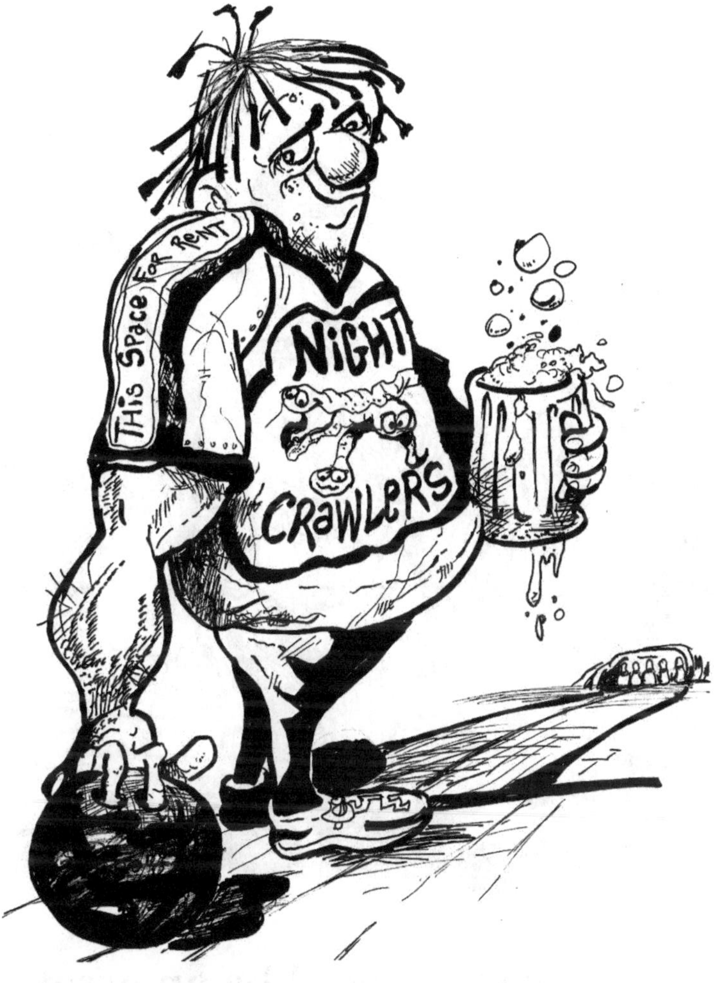
THis Space FOR RENT
NiGHT
CRaWLeRS

"I love BEER FRAMES!"

"Your son would be an asset
for my team."

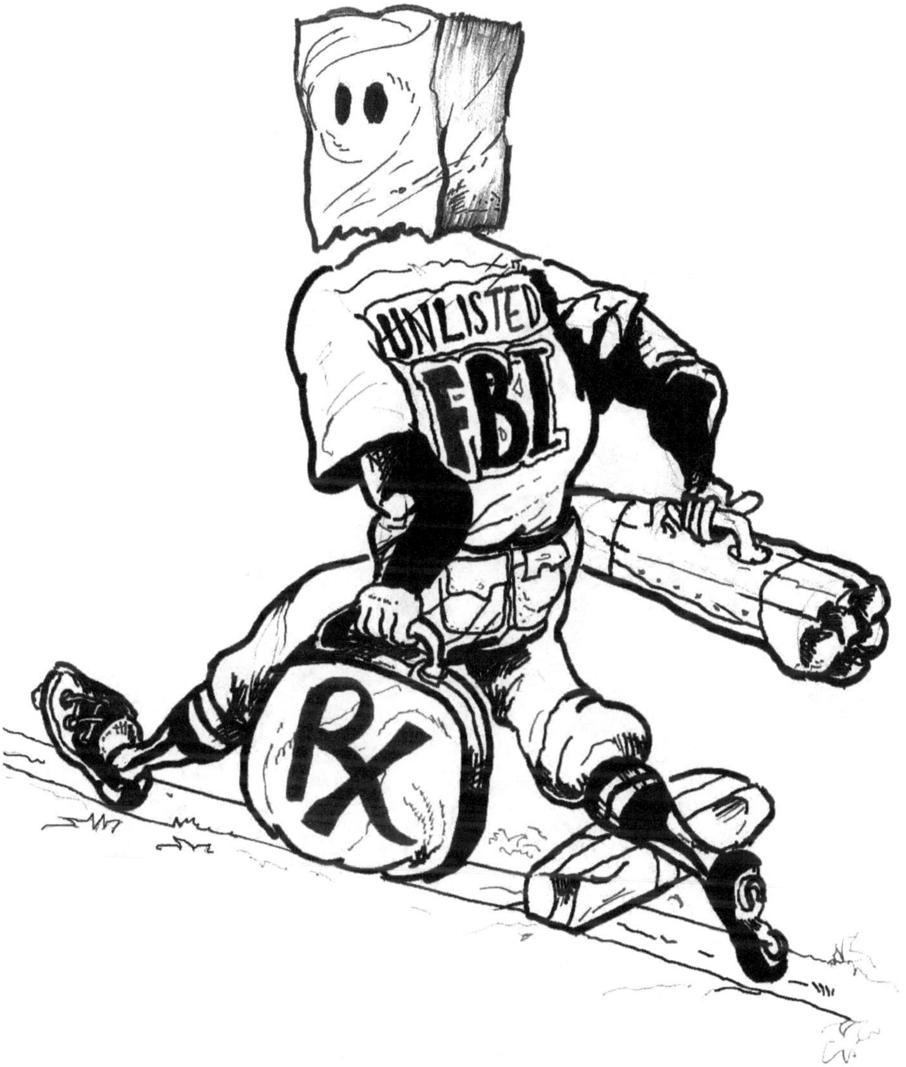
UNLISTED
FBI
RX

Running away from home

**"I should have taken up
tennis instead of golf!"**

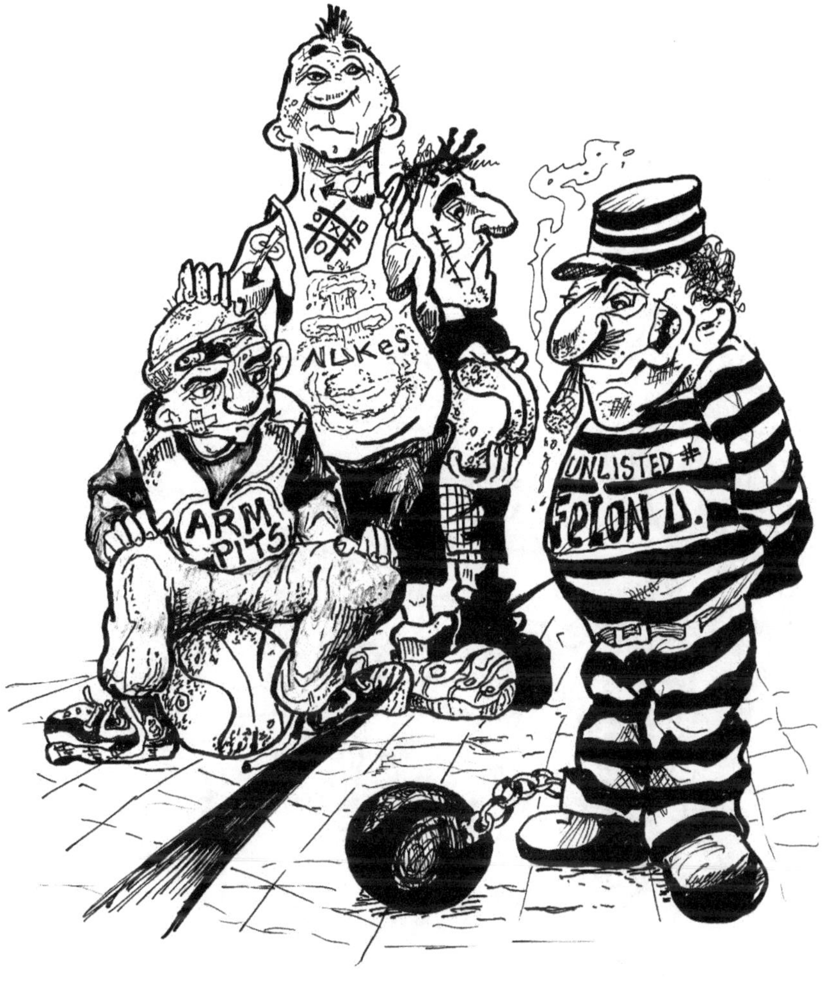
NUKES
ARM PITS
UNLISTED #
FELON U.

"I'd like to see you play basketball with this ball and chain around your ankle."

"The worse shot in golf is when you're standing too close to the ball AFTER you hit it!"

"Actually, they're temporary tattoos!"

"I play tennis because I am NOT
old enough to play golf!"

"You said we should "TOUCH BASE" sometime!"

"Which one are we?
The "x's" or the "o's"?"

"MASCOT SUMMER CAMP"

SOME
ASSEMBLY
REQUIRED
GOAL
LINE
STAND

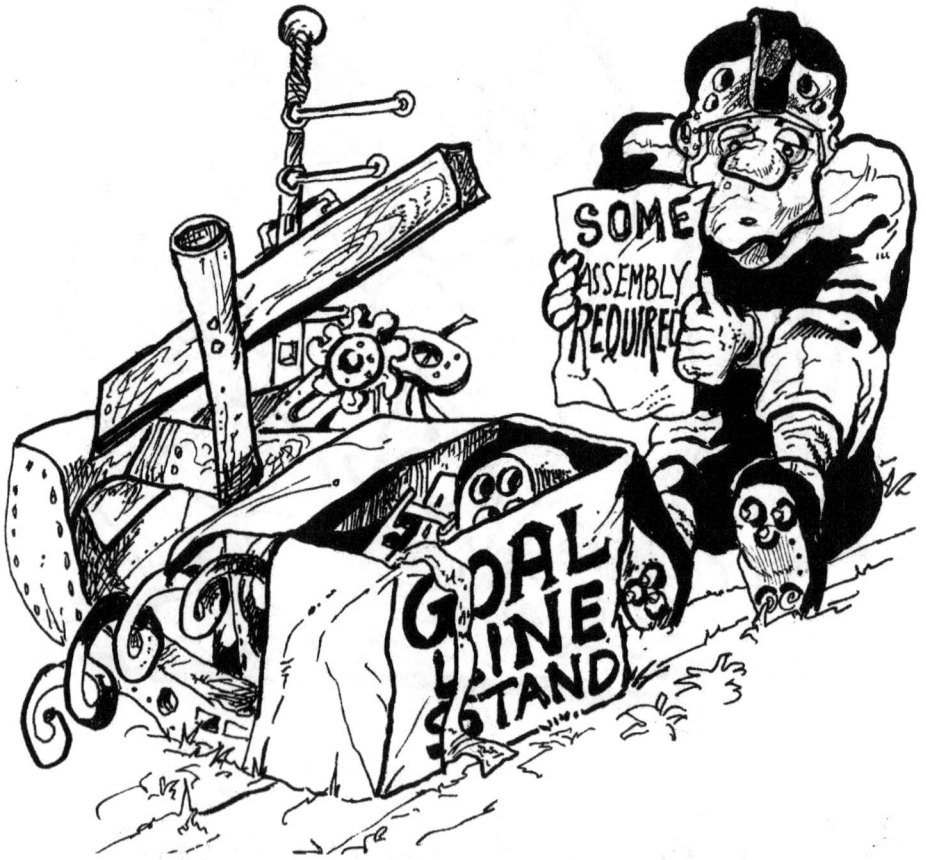

www.ingramcontent.com/pod-product-compliance
Lightning Source LLC
Chambersburg PA
CBHW060647030426
42337CB00018B/3488